SALT AND LIGHT
POCKET GUIDES

COMING TO
GRIPS WITH
DEATH
AND
DYING

D1234059

COMING TO GRIPS WITH
DEATH AND DYING

ERWIN W. LUTZER

MOODY PRESS
CHICAGO

All Scripture quotations, unless noted other-
wise, are from the *New American Standard Bible*, © 1960, 1962, 1963, 1968, 1971, 1972,
1973, 1975, and 1977 by The Lockman Foun-
dation, and are used by permission.

ISBN: 0-8024-3585-8

1 3 5 7 9 10 8 6 4 2

Printed in the United States of America

Coming to Grips with
DEATH AND DYING

During the last few months of her struggle with cancer, Jacquelyn Helton kept a diary. Her thoughts and feelings would become a legacy for her husband, Tom, and her eighteen-month-old daughter, Jennifer.

In her diary she wonders what death would be like. What clothes should she wear for burial? She thinks of her daughter. *Who will love her? Put her to sleep?* In her writings she tells Jennifer that when it hurts she should remember that her mother would have cared. Then she thinks of her husband and the needs he will have after she is gone.

Finally she cries out, "What is the matter with you, God? My family is not a bunch of Boy Scouts who can figure all these things out for themselves—you're some kind of idiot to pull something like this!"[1]

Denial, anger, fear, depression, and helpless resignation—all of these

5

feelings erupt in the souls of those who face death. No matter that death is common to the human race; each person must face this ultimate humiliation individually. Friends and family can walk only as far as the curtain; the dying one must disappear behind the veil alone.

Tom Howard says that when we face death we are like a hen before a cobra, incapable of doing anything at all in the presence of the very thing that seems to call for the most drastic and decisive action. "There is, in fact, nothing we can do," he writes. "Say what we will, dance how we will, we will soon enough be a heap of ruined feathers and bones, indistinguishable from the rest of the ruins that lie about. It will not appear to matter in the slightest whether we met the enemy with equanimity, shrieks, or a trumped-up gaiety, *there we will be.*"

Yet, some people believe that the almost universal fear of death is unfounded. When actor Michael Landon, of TV's "Little House on the Prairie" and "Bonanza," lay on his deathbed, he confided to friends that he saw a "bright white light" that eased his fears and made him look forward to what awaited him on the other side. He died calmly, anticipating what he called "quite an experience."

Hollywood is obsessed with the theme of death. In 1991 at least a dozen movies dealt with the hereafter. Reincarnation, altered states of consciousness, and glad reunions in a metaphysical place such as heaven are popular themes at the box office. Larry Gordon, chief executive of Largo Entertainment, says, "People are looking for something that makes them feel good. We all want to believe that death isn't so bad."[2]

Hell fire has been supplanted by blissful feelings about a hereafter where everyone ends happily reunited. There is no judgment, no careful review of one's life. Death has mystery but is not to be feared. Given this positive assessment of the Great Beyond we should not be surprised that some people want to hasten their arrival at this destination.

This booklet is written to answer several questions about death and dying:

- Is suicide a reasonable option in the face of prolonged emotional or physical suffering?
- How should we interpret the paranormal experiences that seem to confirm life after death?
- How can a Christian receive comfort in view of his/her impending death?
- What role should grief play in dealing with death?

- What can we learn about how to die from Christ's example?

Above all, *Coming to Grips with Death and Dying* is a booklet of hope, a scriptural discussion of how a Christian can witness the faithfulness of God while facing death.

Before we investigate this message of comfort, however, we must expose some false contemporary ideas about the hereafter.

THE DO-IT-YOURSELF APPROACH

The suffering that often precedes death is so excruciating that many people hope to leapfrog over the process of dying to get to death itself. Books explaining how to commit suicide are selling briskly; a growing number of people want to "control their own destinies" rather than be at the mercy of modern medicine.

The best-selling book *Final Exit*, by Derek Humphry, is a death manual loaded with charts of lethal dosages for eighteen prescription drugs and sleeping tablets. It includes information about asphyxiation and auto exhaust. Practical tips on how to make sure no one will suspect that you are taking your life are also included. The author's intention is to help individuals commit suicide without fear of botching the attempt.

One argument for assisting in death is that medical technology has artificially prolonged life. Modern medicine sometimes *has* gone too far in keeping people alive long after any hope of recovery is past. However, the idea that we all have the right to "die with dignity" is based on a false premise. If taken seriously by society in general, it would lead to disastrous consequences.

Strictly speaking, no one "dies with dignity." Ever since sin entered the world and brought death with it, death has always been the final humiliation, the one unalterable fact that confirms our mortality and reduces our bodies (yes, even beautiful ones) to ashes.

Jesus Himself hung on a cross naked, exposed to the gawkers that walked by outside the walls of Jerusalem. Thankfully, none of us will likely have to endure such shameful public torture, but death is never pretty. Death is the ultimate affirmation that we are but dust and to dust we shall return.

Those who choose suicide (for whatever reason) should remember that physical death is not the end, but a doorway to an eternal existence. Sadly, some who find the pain of dying intolerable will awaken in a realm that is even more terrible, more frightening, more hopeless than the dying experienced on earth. For such, suicide is a self-inflicted wound that leads to irreparable alienation from God.

Others, who have become Christians before their early death, shall see heaven. Nonetheless, their suicide remains an act of rebellion against God's will and purpose; it is the final confession of failure.

Suicide is never a sensible option. Those who contemplate this escape should seek immediate help from a pastor, counselor, or friend.

EVIDENCE FOR LIFE AFTER DEATH

There is a growing belief that a moment after we die we will be conscious, experiencing a new dimension of reality. Many are convinced that the immortality of the soul is now confirmed by paranormal experiences that can have no other explanation but that the soul survives the death of the body. Let's carefully weigh the evidence.

THE OCCULT

Some descriptions of life after death come from the occultic realm. In his book *The Other Side*, Bishop Pike described in detail how he made contact with his son who had committed suicide. Using a spirit medium, the bishop had what he believed to be several extensive conversations with the boy.

"I failed the test, I can't face you, can't face life," Pike's son reportedly said. "I'm confused . . . I am not in purgatory, but something like Hell, here . . . yet nobody blames me here."[3] Jesus, the boy said, was an example but not a Savior.

A surprise was the alleged appearance in spirit of a friend, Paul Tillich, a well known German-American theologian who had died several months before. Pike was caught off guard when he discerned his deceased friend's German accent passing through the lips of the medium.

How should this evidence be interpreted? Liberal theologian that he was, Pike did not realize that demons impersonate the dead to create the illusion that the living can communicate with the dead. These spirits have astonishing knowledge of the dead person's life since they carefully observe individuals while they are living. Through the power of deception they can mimic a deceased person's voice, personality, and even appearance. The King James Version of the Bible actually translates the word *medium* as those who have "familiar spirits" (Leviticus 19:31; 20:6, 27; Deuteronomy 18:11), suggesting the

11

familiarity some demons have with individuals.

Although Samuel was apparently brought back from the dead, a more careful reading of the text shows that this miracle was done by God and not the witch at Endor (1 Samuel 28:3-25). This explains the medium's terror (v. 12).

Be assured that no one has ever talked to your dead uncle, cousin, or grandmother. There are, however, spirits that impersonate the dead. Their trickery is compounded because they may actually talk about love, the value of religion, or make favorable references to Christ.

This ability of demonic spirits to masquerade as the personality of the dead helps us understand haunted houses. While I was staying in a hotel near Calgary, a local newspaper carried a story saying that there were at least two ghosts in the beautiful building. One of the employees showed us a marble staircase where one of these ghosts lived (verified by the testimony of employees). A new bride had stumbled down the stairs years ago and hit her head, resulting in her death. We were told that her spirit now lives on the stairs, appearing with some regularity.

How do we explain this phenomenon? When a person who is inhabited by evil spirits dies, these demons need to relocate. Often they choose to stay in the place where the death took place (this seems particularly true in the case of violent deaths such as murder or suicide). They will take the name and characteristics of the deceased person and make occasional appearances under these pretenses. Such entities are evil spirits who often pose as "friendly ghosts."

To try to contact the dead is to invite fellowship with hosts of darkness pretending to be helpful angels of light. Isaiah the prophet warned the people that to consult a medium was to turn one's back on God (Isaiah 8:19,20).

REINCARNATION

Another form of occultism that purports to give information about life after death is reincarnationism. This doctrine teaches that we just keep being recycled; death is nothing more than a transition from one body to another. Thus Shirley MacLaine claims we can eliminate the fear of death by proclaiming that it does not exist. Through contacts in the spirit world, she has discovered that in a previous existence she was a princess in Atlantis, an Inca in Peru, and even was a child raised by elephants. In some previous existences she was male, in others female.

A woman I met on a plane told me that as a child she had detailed knowledge of a house in Vermont that she had never visited. Later, as an adult, the accuracy of her visions was confirmed; she discovered that she had lived there in the eighteenth century. I pointed out that there is no such thing as a transmigration of souls, but there is a transmigration of demons. She was getting knowledge about an eighteenth century family from evil spirits.

"But," she protested, "I have nothing to do with evil spirits; I communicate only with good ones!"

"How do you tell the difference between good spirits and evil ones?" I asked.

"I communicate only with those spirits that come to me clothed in light."

I reminded her of 2 Corinthians 11:13,14, "For such men are false apostles, deceitful workers, disguising themselves as apostles of Christ. And no wonder, for even Satan disguises himself as an angel of light." Yes, light indeed!

Her experiences and similar ones do not prove reincarnation, but rather confirm that people of all ages can become the victims of demonic influence. There is evidence that even children sometimes inherit the demonically induced traits of their parents or ancestors. This would explain why some children, a few months old, have reportedly babbled blasphemies and obscenities that they could never have learned personally in their short life.

Occultism, of whatever variety, is not a reliable source of information regarding what happens after death. It proves only the existence of a spirit world, a world of deception and dark intelligence. God considers all forms of occultism an abomination (see the strong condemnations in Leviticus 19:31; Deuteronomy 18:9-12; Isaiah 8:19-20; 1 Corinthians 10:14-22).

NEAR-DEATH EXPERIENCES

A second source of information regarding life after death comes from so-called near-death experiences. In *Life After Life* (Mocking Bird), Raymond Moody recorded the interviews of many who were near death but were successfully resuscitated. Their stories, for the most part, had many similar elements: the patient would hear himself being pronounced dead; he would be out of his body, watching the doctors work over his corpse. While in this state, he would meet relatives or friends who had died and then encounter a "being of light." When he knows that he must return to his body, he does so reluctantly because the experience of love and peace has engulfed him.

Melvin Morse, in his book *Closer to the Light*, recounts the stories of children who have had near death experiences. Their stories are again remarkably similar, and in almost all instances very positive. Typical is the account of a sixteen year old boy who was rushed to the hospital with a severe kidney problem. While in the admitting room, he slumped over in his chair. A nurse searched for his pulse but found none. Thankfully, he was eventually resuscitated. Later he told of a supernatural experience:

> I reached a certain point in the tunnel where lights suddenly began flashing all around me. They made me certain that I was in some kind of tunnel, and the way I moved past them, I knew I was going hundreds of miles an hour.
>
> At this point I also noticed that there was somebody with me. He was about seven feet tall and wore a long white gown with a simple belt tied at the waist. His hair was golden, and although he didn't say anything, I wasn't afraid because I could feel him radiating peace and love.
>
> No, he wasn't the Christ, but I knew that he was sent from Christ. It was probably one of his angels or someone else sent to transport me to Heaven.[4]

These near-death experiences are positive and inviting. Other research, however, indicates that many have dark and forboding experiences. In *The Edge of Death*, by Philip J. Swihart, and *Beyond Death's Door*, by Maurice Rawlings, there are accounts of those who tell terrifying stories of the life beyond. Some have seen a lake of fire or abysmal darkness along with tormented persons, all of whom are awaiting judgment. These reports, the authors contend, are more accurate because they were gained through interviews almost immediately after near death and resuscitation. These dark experiences apparently are often lost to the memory after a short period of time.

What do these experiences prove? Apparently, they do confirm that at death the soul separates from the body. A few patients not only looked back and saw doctors hover around their body, but could see what was happening in other places in the hospital. This, it seems, is impossible unless the soul had actually left the body and could review earth from a different perspective.

But let us remember that these experiences may or may not reflect the true conditions of life beyond death. For that we need a more reliable guide. Christians believe that near-death experiences must be carefully evaluated to see whether they conform to the biblical picture of the hereafter. Some experiences may provide a glimpse of the other side, others may be misleading.

We have reason to believe that a person may see Christ in the twilight zone between life and death. Before Stephen was stoned God gave him a glimpse into heaven. He said, "Behold I see the heavens opened up and the Son of man standing at the right hand of God" (Acts 7:56). Though Stephen was not physically ill (the stones had not yet begun to fly), he was given this special revelation of the spirit world. Here was positive encouragement that Heaven was waiting to receive him.

If Stephen saw our Lord, other believers might also have such a vision. Paul the apostle himself had a vision in which he was caught up to the third heaven (2 Corinthians 12:3-5). But let us remember that Satan would want to give the same positive experience to unbelievers. The Great Deceiver wants people to think a relationship with Jesus Christ cannot affect the beauty and bliss that awaits everyone.

We know that at least some positive near death experiences are demonic because they sharply contradict the teaching of the Bible. First, some who encounter death say that everyone will have an equally blissful welcome into the life beyond. Second, we are told that there is no judgment, no rigorous examination of a person's life. Several of the people explicitly mention that the "being" they met gives everyone an unconditional welcome.

One woman reported that when she crossed the line between life and death she met Christ, who explained that all the religions of the world were paths to the same destination. There was a Buddhist path, a Hindu path, a Muslim path, and of course a Christian path. But like spokes in a wheel, all of them led to the central hub of heaven. In other words, everyone will be saved. This, as always, has been Satan's most believable lie.

Personally, I am much more concerned about what I will experience *after* death than what I will experience when I am *near* death. It's not the transition but the destination that really counts. Thus, to find out what really lies on the other side, we must go to a more reliable map, a more certain authority than people who go only to the threshold of the life beyond.

We will do much better if we trust someone who actually was dead, not someone who was just near death. Christ was dead, so dead that His body became cold and was put into a tomb. Three days later He was raised from the dead with a glorified body. To John, this risen Christ said, "Do not be afraid; I am the first and the last, and the living One; and I was dead, and behold, I am alive forevermore, and I have the keys of death and Hades" (Revelation 1:17*b*, 18).

THE BIBLE ON LIFE AFTER DEATH

We now turn from the limitations of human experience to the clear teaching of the Bible. Yes, there is life after death. And no, it is not a pleasant experience for everyone.

Death originated when Adam and Eve rebelled against the direct command of God. Our first parents were free to eat from any tree of the garden, "but from the tree of the knowledge of good and evil you shall not eat, for in the day that you eat from it you shall surely die" (Genesis 2:17).

Death is proof that God judges sin. On that fateful day in Eden, Adam and Eve died *spiritually* in that they were separated from God and tried to hide from Him. They also began to die *physically*, as their bodies began the journey to the grave. And if Adam and Eve had not been redeemed by God, they would have died *eternally*, which is the third form of death. From disobedience in Eden, death in all of its forms began its trek throughout the world.

But a blessing is concealed behind the terror of death. When God provided the clothes of animals for Adam and Eve, He was signaling His intention to redeem at least a part of the human race. The Redeemer would crush the head of the serpent and the apparent advantage Satan had would only be temporary.

SHEOL AND HELL

In the Old Testament the Hebrew word Sheol referred to the place of the dead. The KJV translates it "the grave" thirty-one times, "hell" thirty times, and "the pit" three times.

Scholars disagree about whether it refers to the place of the unbelieving dead or a place where all men went at death. The problem is that both good men (such as Jacob) and bad men (such as Korah and Dathan) go there. This led the early church to believe that there were two compartments in Sheol, one for the righteous and the other for the wicked.

Others believe that Sheol simply means the grave, and thus refers only to the destination of the body. The destiny of the soul is found by appealing to other passages of Scripture that speak of the afterlife. Although in the Old Testament the fate of the wicked and righteous is not always clearly distinguished, some passages do contrast the separate destinies of believers and unbelievers. (See Psalms 49:14, 15; 9:17; 16:10; 31:17; 55:15; Job 24:19; Daniel 12:2.)

If the door to the afterlife is open but a crack in the Old Testament, it swings wide open in the New. Here we have detailed descriptions of both the righteous and the wicked after death. The contrast is between everlasting bliss and everlasting damnation.

Jesus told the story of a rich man who died and whose soul was taken to hades; meanwhile a beggar named Lazarus who had lain at the rich man's gate also died and was carried into Abraham's bosom (apparently another term for heaven or paradise). Christ's description of the hereafter is revealing:

> And in Hades he lifted up his eyes being in torment, and saw Abraham far away and Lazarus in his bosom. And he cried out and said, "Father Abraham, have mercy on me and send Lazarus that he may dip the tip of his finger in water and cool off my tongue; for I am in agony in this flame."
>
> But Abraham said "Child, remember that during your life you received good things and likewise Lazarus bad things; but now he is

being comforted here and you are in agony. And besides all this between us and you there is a great chasm fixed in order that those who wish to come over from here to you may not be able, and that none may cross over from there to us." (Luke 16:23-26)

Notice that both men were fully conscious immediately after death. Memory, speaking, pain, and bliss —all of these were a part of their experience. Some interpreters teach the doctrine of "soul sleep," that is, that the soul is unconscious at death and "sleeps" until the day of resurrection. But this story, along with other passages of Scripture, contradicts this theory.

Paul was so anxious to see Christ that he preferred death to life. "We are of good courage, I say, and prefer rather to be absent from the body and to be at home with the Lord" (2 Corinthians 5:8). He knew that death meant instant transport of his soul to the presence of God in heaven. Christ assured the thief on the cross that they would meet in paradise that very day (Luke 23:43).

NO EXIT

In addition, the two men's eternal destinies were irrevocably fixed. "Between us and you there is a great chasm fixed in order that those who wish to come over from here to you may not be able and that none may cross over from there to us." At death our destination can never be changed.

Christ's account also reveals that godless man faces isolation and final judgment. The rich man was not yet in hell, but hades. Even now as I write this booklet on my computer, this man is still in hades awaiting final judgment in hell. Those who have not come under the protection of Christ's sacrifice must bear the full weight of their sin alone.

Hades is not purgatory. The doctrine of purgatory is not found in the Bible but was accepted as a tradition in medieval times because of a faulty doctrine of salvation. The belief was that nobody (or almost nobody) was righteous enough to enter into heaven at death, thus there must be a place where men and women are purged from their sins to prepare them for heavenly bliss. Purgatory, the theory went, may last for millions of years (depending on the level of righteousness one has attained), but eventually it would come to an end.

Although purgatory does not exist, Hades does and it has no exit; eventually it will be thrown into the lake of fire. As Dante wrote, "Abandon all hope ye who enter here!" (The final section of this booklet,"Your Assurance of Heaven," tells how to avoid this terrible fate.)

Death, then, has two faces: to the unbeliever it is the doorway to eternal damnation. But for those who have made their peace with God, death is a blessing; it is a means of redemption, a doorway into a blissful eternity. Paul included death among the possessions of the Christian, "For all things belong to you, whether Paul or Apollos or Cephas or the world or life or death or things present or things to come; all things belong to you, and you belong to Christ; and Christ belongs to God" (1 Corinthians 3:21-23).

Every human person is in the process of becoming a noble being; noble beyond imagination. Or else, alas, a vile being, evil beyond redemption, writes C.S. Lewis. He exhorts us "to remember that the dullest and most uninteresting person you talk to may one day be a creature which, if you saw it now, you would be strongly tempted to worship, or else a horror and a corruption such as you now meet, if at all, only in a nightmare. There are no *ordinary* people . . . . It is immortals who we joke with, work with, marry, snub and exploit—immortal horrors or everlasting splendors."[5]

Thus the race stands divided between those who die under the protection of Christ and those who will stand before God on the strength of their own flawed performance.

FACING THE FINAL MOMENTS

For the Christian, death is God's servant used to transport His people from earth to Heaven. Christ died that He "might deliver those who through fear of death were subject to slavery all of their lives" (Hebrews 2:15).

Little wonder Paul wrote, "O death, where is your victory? O death, where is your sting?" (1 Corinthians 15:55). A bee can sting a man only once. Although the insect can still frighten us when the stinger is gone, if we know the truth we need have no fear. Because Christ removed death's sting, it can only threaten; it cannot make good on its threats.

When facing death, we can find comfort in hope, peace—and even *good* grief. We need only see that final earthly event as God does. The New Testament uses several figures of speech to help us understand what death truly means for those who know God and His Son, Jesus Christ.

DEATH AS DEPARTURE

First, death is a departure. On the mount of transfiguration Moses and Elijah appeared with Christ and "were speaking of His departure which He was about to accomplish in Jerusalem" (Luke 9:31). In Greek the word *departure* is *exodus*, the name of the second book of the Old Testament that gives the details regarding the exit of the children of Israel from Egypt.

Just as Moses led his people out of slavery, so now Christ passed through the iron gates of death so that He can safely conduct us from earth to Heaven.

There was nothing fearful about taking the journey from Egypt to Canaan; the people simply had to follow Moses the servant of God. Neither is it fearful for us to make our exodus, for we are following our leader who has gone on ahead. When the curtain parts, we shall find Him waiting on the other side.

A little girl was asked whether she feared walking through the cemetery. She replied, "No, I'm not afraid, for my home is on the other side!"

DEATH AS SLEEP

Second, death is likened to sleep. When Christ entered the home of the ruler of the synagogue, He comforted the crowd by saying that his daughter was not dead but sleeping (Luke 8:52). Then as He began His trip to Bethany He said to the disciples, "Our friend Lazarus has fallen asleep; but

27

I go, that I may awaken him out of sleep" (John 11:11).

Paul used the same figure of speech when he taught that some believers would not see death but would be caught up to meet Christ. "Behold, I tell you a mystery; we shall not all sleep, but we shall all be changed" (1 Corinthians 15:51). Only the body sleeps; the soul does not.

Sleep is used as a figure of death because it is a means of rejuvenation. We look forward to sleep when we feel exhausted and our work is done. Furthermore, we do not fear falling asleep for we have the assurance that we shall awaken in the morning. Yes, we shall awaken and be more alive than we ever have been!

"Blessed are the dead who die in the Lord from now on . . . that they may rest from their labors, for their deeds follow with them" (Revelation 14:13). Rest at last!

A COLLAPSING TENT

Paul spoke of death as the dismantling of a tent. "For we know that if the earthly tent which is our house is torn down, we have a building from God, a house not made with hands, eternal in the Heavens" (2 Corinthians 5:1).

Our present body is like a tent where our spirit dwells; it is a temporary structure. Tents deteriorate in the face of changing weather and storms. A tattered tent is a sign that we will soon have to move. Death takes us from the tent to the palace; it is changing our address from earth to heaven.

To the terrified disciples Christ said, "Let not your heart be troubled; believe in God, believe also in Me. In My Father's house are many dwelling places; if it were not so, I would have told you; for I go to prepare a place for you. And if I go and prepare a place for you I will come again, and receive you to Myself; that where I am, there you may be also" (John 14:1-3).

A tent reminds us that we are only pilgrims here on earth, enroute to our final home. Someone has said that we should not drive in our stakes too deeply for we are leaving in the morning!

DEATH AS A SAILING SHIP

Finally, Paul speaks of death as the sailing of a ship. He wrote, "But I am hard-pressed from both directions, having the desire to depart and to be with Christ, for that is very much better" (Philippians 1:23). That word *depart* was used for the loosing of an anchor. A. T. Robertson translates it, "To weigh anchor and put out to sea."

29

Thanks to Christ, Paul was ready to embark on this special journey that would take him to his heavenly destination. Christ had already successfully navigated to the other side and was waiting with a host of Paul's friends. Of course, he had some friends on this side too; that's why he added, "Yet to remain on in the flesh is more necessary for your sake" (v.24).

Paul's bags were packed, he was ready to go. But for now the Captain said, "Wait!" A few years later Paul was closer to leaving earth's shore. Again he spoke of death as his departure, "For I am already being poured out as a drink offering, and the time of my departure has come" (2 Timothy 4:6). The signal for him to push off was imminent. He said "goodbye," but only for the time being. He would not return to Timothy, but Timothy, would soon cross over and they would meet again.

John Drummond tells the story of a sea captain who was asked to visit a dying man in a hospital. When the captain reached the sick man's room he noticed decorated flags of different colors surrounding his bed. As they talked the captain learned that both of them had actually served on the same ship many years earlier.

"What do these flags mean?" the captain wondered.

"Have you forgotten the symbols?" the dying man asked.

Then he continued. "These flags mean that the ship is ready to sail and is awaiting orders" the dying man replied.

Our flags must always be flying for we know neither the day nor the hour of our departure. Some are given more notice than others, but all must go when the Celestial Clock strikes.

But will we have grace to face our exit victoriously? I have not had to face my own imminent death, nor have there been any recent deaths in our immediate family. I can't predict how I might react if I were told that I have a terminal disease.

I, for one, would like to have dying grace long before I need it! But the famous English preacher Charles Haddon Spurgeon says that death is the last enemy to be destroyed and we should leave him to the last. He adds,

> Brother, you do not want dying grace till dying moments. What would be the good of dying grace while you are yet alive? A boat will only be needful when you reach a river. Ask for living grace, and glorify Christ thereby, and then you shall have dying grace when the dying time comes.

Your enemy is going to be destroyed but not today.... Leave the final shock of arms till the last adversary advances, and meanwhile hold your place in the conflict. God will in due time help you to overcome your last enemy, but meanwhile see to it that you overcome the world, the flesh and the devil.[6]

Some believers who thought they could not face death discovered they had the strength to die gracefully when their time came. The same God who guides us on earth will escort us all the way to Heaven. "With Thy counsel Thou wilt guide me, And afterward receive me to glory" (Psalm 73:24).

GOOD GRIEF

Dying grace does not mean that we will be free from sorrow, whether at our own impending death or the death of someone we love. Some Christians have mistakenly thought that grief demonstrates a lack of faith. Thus they have felt it necessary to maintain strength rather than deal honestly with a painful loss.

Good grief is grief that enables us to make the transition to a new phase of existence. The widow must learn to live alone; the parents must bear the loneliness brought on by the death of a child. Grief that deals honestly with the pain is a part of the healing process. Christ wept at the tomb of Lazarus and agonized with "loud crying and tears" in Gethsemane at His own impending death (Hebrews 5:7).

Some Christians have thought that there should be no sorrow at funerals; only rejoicing should be expected. How contrary this is to the teaching of the Bible! Dozens of passages in the Old and New Testament tell how the saints mourned. When Stephen, the first Christian martyr, was stoned we read, "And some devout men buried Stephen, and made loud lamentations over him" (Acts 8:2).

Let those of us who wish to comfort the sorrowing remember that words can have a hollow ring for those who are overwhelmed with grief. Let us by our presence "weep with those who weep" (Romans 12:15). We must say we care much louder with our actions than with our words.

As Christians we live with the tension between what is already ours and the "not yet" of our experience. Paul said believers should look forward to Christ's return "that you may not grieve, as do the rest who have no hope" (1 Thessalonians 4:13). Grief was expected, but it is different from the grief of the world. There is a difference between tears of hope and tears of hopelessness.

A Lesson in How to Die

What attitude should a Christian have toward death? Cancer, accidents, and a hundred different diseases lurk about waiting for an opportunity to devour us. Death awaits us, as the concrete floor awaits the falling light bulb.

Christ is our best example of how to face the final hour that will come to us all. He died so that we could die triumphantly. Through death Christ "rendered powerless him who had the power of death, that is, the devil; and might deliver those who through fear of death were subject to slavery all their lives" (Hebrews 2:14b-15).

When we understand the reality of the life beyond we will never have to say of a believer "he has departed." Rather, he has arrived! Heaven is the Christian's final destination. Thanks to Christ we can be free from the fear of death. We can understand how to face death as we notice how Jesus faced death.

DYING WITH THE RIGHT ATTITUDE

First, He died with the right attitude. Christ died with a mixture of grief and joy. In Gethsemane He declared, "My soul is deeply grieved to the point of death; remain here and keep watch with Me" (Matthew 26:28). The disciples failed him, so alone He

34

pleaded with His Father, "My Father, if this cannot pass away unless I drink it, Thy will be done" (v. 42).

He agonized as He contemplated becoming identified with the sins of the world. He would soon become legally guilty of adultery, theft, and murder. As the sin bearer, He knew that His personal holiness would come in contact with the defilement of sin. He was sorrowful unto death as He wrestled with the trauma that awaited Him.

But there was hope too. His impending death was a doorway leading back to the Father; it was the path to victory. Moments before He went to Gethsemane, He said, "And now, glorify Thou Me together with Thyself, Father, with the glory which I had with Thee before the world was" (John 17:5). We read elsewhere that He endured the cross "for the joy set before Him . . . despising the shame, and has sat down at the right hand of the throne of God" (Hebrews 12:2). For the short term there was pain; but long term, there was glory and joy.

We should not feel guilty about facing death with apprehension, for Christ Himself experienced emotional agony the night before the horror of the cross. Yet, with the fear came comfort; joy and sorrow existed in the same heart. Death was, after all, the Father's will for Christ, and for us all.

35

A daughter said of her godly father who died of cancer, "In his closing days, Dad spent more time in heaven than he did on earth." If we can look beyond the immediate heartache to the eventual glory, there is joy. The exit is grievous; the entrance is joyful.

DYING AT THE RIGHT TIME

Second, He died at the right time. The night of His betrayal Christ chose to eat the passover with His disciples. "Now before the Feast of the Passover, Jesus, knowing that His hour had come that He should depart out of this world to the Father, having loved His own who were in the world, He loved them to the end" (John 13:1).

This was the hour into which was compacted the agony of Gethsemane, the betrayal of Judas, and the excruciating death of the cross. Interestingly, three times before this we read that His hour had not come (John 2:4; 7:30; 8:20). Until "the hour" arrived His enemies were powerless against Him.

What sustained Christ? We read, "Jesus, knowing that the Father had given all things into His hands, and that He had come forth from God, and was going back to God, rose from supper, and laid aside His garments; and taking a towel, He girded Himself about" (John 13:3-4).

He had come to earth at an hour appointed by God and now He was returning on schedule. There was not the slightest possibility that Christ would die sooner than God planned.

Christ died during Passover, just as God intended, a striking reminder that He was indeed "the lamb of God who takes away the sin of the world" (John 1:29). He was only thirty-three, young by today's standards and those of ancient Middle Eastern culture. Why not fifty-three so that He could have many more years of healing the sick and preaching the love of God to the multitudes?

But though He died young, His work was finished. *You and I don't have to live a long life to do all that God has planned for us to do.* Some of God's best servants have died at an early age—early from our standpoint, on time from God's.

The death of a child seems like mockery since God is taking a life before he/she has the joy of accomplishment. As Jung says, "It is like putting a period before the end of the sentence."

But a child's short life can fulfill the will of God. Though we do not understand it, that little one has also "finished the work God has given him/her to do."

Jim Elliot, who himself was killed at a young age while doing missionary work among the Indians of Ecuador, said, "God is peopling Heaven, why should He limit Himself to old people?"

Why, indeed! If the Almighty wants to reach down and take one of His little lambs, or if He wishes to take a servant in the prime of life, He has that right. We think it cruel only because we cannot see behind the dark curtain.

Our death is just as meticulously planned as the death of Christ. Evil men, disease, or accident cannot come to us as long as God has work for us to do. We die according to God's timetable and not ours.

Christ's own death was brought about by the vicious actions of evildoers. The apostle Peter explains the crime as part of God's good plan: "For truly in this city there were gathered together against Thy holy servant Jesus, whom Thou didst anoint, both Herod and Pontius Pilate, along with the Gentiles and the peoples of Israel, to do whatever Thy hand and Thy purpose predestined to occur" (Acts 4:27,28). They could not act until God's clock struck. The "hour" had to come.

If the violent and unjust death of Christ was part of God's meticulous plan, we can be confident that our own death is equally a part of God's design. No believer who walks with

God dies until his work is finished, until his "hour" has come.

DYING THE RIGHT WAY

He died in the right way. There are many ways to die: disease, accidents, murder, to name a few. The circumstances differ for each individual. In God's plan, Christ was to die on a cross, for this was a symbol of humiliation and an unmistakable sign that He was cursed by God. It was death without dignity.

Today most people are able to die under heavy sedation so that their exit is made as peaceful as possible. When Christ was offered wine mingled with myrrh, He refused this ancient sedative so that He could die with all of his senses fully aware of His surroundings. He took all the horror that death could offer.

If Christ, who was brutally murdered by jealous religious leaders, died as planned by God, why should we think that a believer who is gunned down in a robbery is any less under the care of the Almighty? Car accidents, heart attacks, cancer—all of these are the means used to open heaven to the children of God. The immediate cause of our death is neither haphazard or arbitrary. The one who knows the number of hairs on our heads and sees the sparrow fall has the destiny of every one of our days in His loving hands.

Little wonder Christ could say, "And do not fear those who kill the body, but are unable to kill the soul; but rather fear Him who is able to destroy both soul and body in hell" (Matthew 10:28). If we fear God, we need fear nothing else.

DYING FOR THE RIGHT PURPOSE

Death always has a divine purpose. God does not let life simply slip away. His Son, Jesus, did not die in tragedy. Within the will of God, His death accomplished redemption for the people whom God had chosen. When He cried, "It is finished," the work was complete.

Our death also has a divine purpose. Obviously, our death does not accomplish redemption, but it is the means by which we finally experience the redemption Christ accomplished for us. Death is the doorway by which we can leave the limitations and pains of this existence and enter into the heavenly realm.

Although we can be thankful for the wonders of modern medicine, there does come a time when believers must answer the call to "come up higher." So often when a Christian becomes ill, we immediately pray for his or her physical restoration. How can we be so sure that it is not God's time to have the person enter into the inheritance that is reserved for him (I Peter 1:4)?

When a person has lived a long life and has virtually no hope of recovery, we must simply commit him to God rather than use heroic measures to eke out one more day of pitiful existence. The day of our death is the day of our glorification. Death is the grand entrance, the door that swings into eternity. Eventually it will open in God's time and God's way to let another child come home where he/she belongs.

DYING WITH THE RIGHT COMMITMENT

Death can be a time of trust in God's deliverance. Christ's last comment was "Father, into thy hands I commit my spirit" (Luke 23:46); thus He died entrusting Himself to the Father whom He so passionately loved.

Many Christians believe that Christ descended into hell (or more accurately hades) before He went to the Father. This teaching has been reinforced by the Apostles' Creed, which says "he descended into hell." But until A.D. 650 no version of the creed included this phrase. The only version before this date that includes it gave the meaning "he descended into the grave." Support for the idea

41

that He did enter hades is found in Acts 2:27, a quotation from Psalm 16:10. But many scholars believe that the Old Testament word *sheol* and the New Testament translation *hades* refer simply to the grave or death. This sense is preferable because the context emphasizes the fact that Christ's body rose from the grave as opposed to David's body, which remained in the grave.

I believe that Christ's soul went immediately to God. To the thief hanging on His left Christ said, "Today you shall be with me in paradise" (Luke 23:43). Together they enjoyed the beauty of heaven on that very day. Three days later Christ was raised from the dead with a glorified body and later ascended into heaven.

To summarize: Although the *immediate* cause of Christ's death was the decision of the religious/political leaders, Christ knew the *ultimate* cause was God. "But the Lord was pleased to crush him, putting Him to grief" (Isaiah 53:10).

Before his death, John Calvin had the same confidence when he said, "Thou Lord bruiseth me. But I am abundantly satisfied since it is from Thy hand."

Death can steal nothing from a Christian. Health, wealth, and joy—all of these come in greater abundance when the spirit goes to God.

This booklet has emphasized that there are two classes of people, those who have come to trust in the righteousness of Christ and those who will some day stand before God on their own record, those who will stand before the holiness and wrath of God without the protection that Christ affords.

Christ's sacrifice on the cross was so complete that those who trust Him are immediately fitted for Heaven. This act of trust on our part must include an admission of our own helplessness; a confession that we are sinners unable to save ourselves, unable to even contribute to our salvation.

Then we must see the completed work of the cross: Christ's payment for sinners was absolutely perfect. These benefits are credited to those who believe. "But as many as received Him, to them He gave the right to become children of God, even to those who believe in His name" (John 1:12).

Here is a prayer you can use to make your trust in Christ personal and final:

Dear God,

I realize that I am a sinner and I can do nothing to save myself. I admit that all of my attempts to earn your favor are futile; forgive me for trusting in rituals and my own attempts at human goodness. I am grateful that Christ died on the cross for sinners like me. Right now I transfer all of my trust to Him for my forgiveness and acceptance before you. On the basis of your promises I receive Christ as my personal Savior and believe you will receive me into heaven. Thank you for accepting me into your family. Amen.

Strictly speaking, if your have trusted Christ, you are already in heaven! Paul says believers have been raised with Christ and are "seated in the heavenlies in Christ Jesus" (Ephesians 2:6). Because we have already established residence in heaven, we need have no fear when we cross the border into our eternal home.

Death is God's will for you and me. It is a dark doorway that leads to eternal light. Thankfully Christ came so that we do not have to walk behind the parted curtain alone.

Notes

1. Jacquelyn Helton died from cancer months after exclaiming her anger. Her story was reported in an edition of the *Chicago Tribune*.
2. Martha Smilgis, "Hollywood Goes to Heaven," *Time*, June 3, 1991, p.70.
3. James A. Pike and Diane Kennedy, *The Other Side* (New York: Doubleday, 1968), p. 115.
4. Melvin Morse, *Closer to the Light* (New York: Ivy, 1990), p. 33.
5. C. S. Lewis, *The Weight of Glory* (Grand Rapids: Eerdmans, 1947), p. 15.
6. "Death Be Not Hurried: Charles Spurgeon's Counsel on Dying Grace," *Eternity*, February 1976, p.14

Books in the Salt and Light series: